Michael and Eric S

CODING
PYTHON

The Ultimate Tool to Progress Your Python
Programming from Good to Great While
Making Coding in Scratch Look Easy

© Copyright 2020 - All rights reserved.

Table of Contents

Introduction

The following chapters will discuss all of the different parts of learning how to do some of your coding in the Python language. There are a lot of different reasons why you will want to learn how to work with the Python language, and we want to make sure that we can take a few steps from the different parts and learn how to make them work for our needs. There are a lot of options out there for learning how to code and get things done with programming, but you will find that the Python language is going to be one of the best ones to work with, and this guidebook will show you why that is.

So, if you think that you want to learn how to program in Python, how to build the next big app, you've come to the right place. This book is intended to give you the basics of programming in Python, a starting point from which you can build your knowledge and your expertise. I have also included some basic projects for you to get started on as well as a few exercises for you to test your knowledge. By the end of the book, you should have a good grounding in what Python is and what it can do.

There are a lot of reasons why you will love working with the Python code.

Python is a programming language that is often recommended for beginners to try messing up things and falling in love with programming. One of the major reasons for the widespread popularity of Python is its simplicity and the power of making things done with less code. Even after the entrance of tens of programming languages in the past decade python doesn't lose its charm, and we are pretty confident that it is going to stay.

Chapter 1:

What's Python?

Python is what is known as object-oriented programming or OOP for short. It is an interpreted language highly interactive and is perfect for beginners or for those who are experienced in other programming languages. Indeed, those who have learned to program in C language will spot straight away that there are an awful lot of similarities between C and Python.

The highlights of this language include:

- Easy to read.

- Easy to learn.

- Easy maintenance.

- An excellent standard library.

- Fully interactive.

- Portable and extendable.

- Packed with databases.

- Excellent GUI programming.

Python is used for so many things and today, it is one of the most popular and important of all the open-source programming languages.

Some see it as a relatively new language, but in fact, Python is older than Java and JavaScript. So, where did it come from?

History of Python

The origins of Python go back to December 1989. The creator was Guido van Rossum, and it was begun as a hobby. Rather than being named after the constrictor snake, Python actually got its name from Monty Python's Flying Circus, the famous British comedy troupe of the eighties.

It came from a project that van Rossum worked on at the Dutch CWI research institute—the ABC language—a project that was terminated and from the Amoeba operating system. The main strength of the new language was the ease of which it was easy to extend and that it could support multiple platforms. This was vital in the days when personal computers were starting to become popular and because Python could communicate with a wide variety of libraries and file formats, it soon took off. Throughout the nineties, Python grew and more functional programming tools were added. It also played a pivotal role in van Rossum's new initiative, Computer Programming for everybody. The idea behind CP4E was to make programming accessible to everybody, not just the selected few, and to encourage basic computer and coding literacy as essential skills besides those of English and math. Because Python has such a clean syntax and is easy to read and access, it is now the language of choice for beginners.

Open-Source Python

Throughout the nineties, as Python continued growing, users were concerned that it was entirely dependent on van Rossum keeping it going. What would happen to Python if something happened to van Rossum?

The solution was to make Python open-source, available to all, and to facilitate that Python 2.0 was released in 2000 by the BeOpen Python Labs team, with the idea of making it more community-oriented and a lot more transparent in the development process. Its repository was moved over to SourceForge, giving more people "Write" access to the CVS tree and a much easier way for bugs to be reported and patches submitted. Today, we still use Python 2.7 and it will continue to receive support until 2020. Indeed, there will be no 2.8; instead, the focus will be on Python 3, the new member of the family.

Python 3

Python 3 was finally born in 2008, not just an update but a complete overhaul. Surprisingly, there would be no backward compatibility, which meant developers would have to choose and use just one. With Python 3, the idea was to clean up the house to remove duplicate models and constructions and ensure that there was one obvious way of doing something. Despite the introduction of tools like "2to3," which would identify things in Python 2 code that had to be changed to work in Python 3, many users opted to stick with what they knew best. Even today, many years after Python 3 was released, there should be no assumption made that programmers would be using the later version.

Chapter 2:

Why Learn Python?

Why Use Python?

The neat thing about working with Python is that it has something for everyone to enjoy along the way. There are tons of benefits that come with it and it really does not matter if you have worked with programming in the past or not.

You will still find something to love about Python, and it is something that is easy to work with for all levels of programming. Some of the different reasons why you may want to work with the Python language overall include:

- **It has some code that is maintainable and readable.** While you are writing out some of the applications for the software, you will need to focus on the quality of source code to simplify some of the updates and the maintenance. The syntax rules of Python are going to allow you a way to express the concepts without having to write out any additional codes. At the same time, Python, unlike some of the other coding languages out there, is going to emphasize the idea of the readability of the code and can allow us to work with keywords in English instead of working with different types of punctuations for that work.

- **Comes with many programming paradigms.** Another benefit that we will see is the multiple programming paradigms. Like some of the other coding languages that we can find, Python is going to support more than one programming paradigm inside of it. This is going to be a language that can support structured and oriented programming to the fullest. In addition, a language will feature some support for various concepts when it comes to functional and aspect-oriented programming.

- **Compatible with most major systems and platforms.** Right now, Python is going to be able to support many different operating systems. It is even possible to work with interpreting to run the code on some of the specific tools and platforms that we want to use. In addition, since this is known as a language that is interpreted, it is going to allow us to go through and run the exact same code on many different platforms without the need to do any recompilation.

- **A very robust standard library.** The standard library that works with Python is robust and has many different parts that go with it. The standard library is a good one to provide us with all of the modules that we need to handle. Each module is further going to enable us to add some of the functionality to the Python application without needing to write out the additional code.

- **It can simplify some of the work that you are doing.** Python is seen as a programming language that is general purpose in nature. This means that you are able to use this language for all of the different processes and programs that you want to, from web applications to developing things like desktop applications as needed. We can even take it further and use this language to help develop complex scientific and numeric applications.

As we can see, some benefits we are able to enjoy when it comes to using the Python language, and this is just the beginning. As we go through and learn more about how to work in this language and what it is able to do for us. We are able to see more and more of the benefits at the same time, and it will not take long working with your own data analysis to understand exactly how great this can be for our needs.

Chapter 3:

Getting Ready for Python

Install Python on Linux

There are two ways to install Python on a Linux system—source installation or package- managed installation. While the latter is preferable, we will discuss both methods:

Package-Managed Installation

The most common method of installing Python on Linux is to use the Linux package systems. This also ensures that you can easily upgrade Python when the time comes. Depending on which distribution of Linux you are using, you will need to use one of these commands:

- **Debian-based, like Ubuntu:** apt-get install python

- **RPM-based, like Red Hat or Fedora:** urpmi python

- **Gentoo:** emerge python

If you don't see the latest version of the installation, you will need to install Python manually, which we will talk about shortly.

You will need to install some extra packages if you want a full installation—these are optional but recommended if you want to be able to profile your programs or have code C extensions. To make sure you have a full installation, install these packages by typing them at the command prompt:

- **Python-dev** – has Python headers for use in compiling C modules.

- **Python-profiler** – has non-GPL modules for use on Debian, Ubuntu, and other full GPL Linux distributions.

- **Gcc** – used for compiling extensions that have C code in them.

Compiling Sources

To do a manual installation, you need to use the cmmi process:

- Configure.

- Make.

- Make install.

This process will perform a Python compilation and then install it on your system.

To get the latest archive for Python, go to http://python.org.download

To perform the download, we use wget with MacPorts or apt— see www.gnu.org/software/wget for more information on your specific distribution.

In order to build Python, we are going to use gcc and make. Make is a program we use to read Makefile configuration files and make sure that all of the requirements are met to compile Python. It is also used as a way of driving the installation and is invoked using the make and configure commands. Gcc is better known as the GNU C Compiler, and it is an open-source compiler that is widely used in building programs. Ensure that both of these have been installed on your Linux system.

To build Python and install it, type in this command at the command prompt:

cd /tmp

wget http://python.org/ftp/python/2.5.1/Python2.5.1.tgz

tar -xzvf tar -xzvf Python2.5.1.tgz

cd Python2.5.1

./configure

make

sudo make install

This also installs all the headers for binary installations that are normally found in python-dev. Once all of this is installed, you should be able to reach Python from the Linux shell.

Install Python on Windows

We can install Python on a Windows system in the same way as a Linux, but this is an incredibly painful way of doing it. Instead, go to http://python.org/downlaod and download the version of Python that you want. All the instructions are provided, making it simple to do. Provided you do not change any of the defaults; you will find Python installed at c:\Python25 and not in the Program Files folder where you would expect to find it. This cuts out the risk of space in the path. Finally, we need to change the PATH environment variable, enabling us to get Python from DOS shell. To do this:

- Find the icon for My Computer on your version of Windows and right-click on it.

- This will open the System Properties dialog box.

- Click on the tab for Advanced.

- Click on the button for Environment Variables.

Edit the PATH system variable to input two new paths, each separated with a semi-colon (;). The paths to be added are:

- c:\Python25 – this will enable python.exe to be called

- c:\Python25\Scripts – this will enable installed third scripts to be called Python should now run in the command prompt.

To open the Run dialog box, press the Windows key and R at the same time. Type cmd in the box and click on Open. At the prompt type in c:/>python, if you see a message like the one below, Python is installed:

Python 2.5.2 (#71, Oct 18 2006, 08:34:43) [MSC v.1310 32 bit (Intel)] on

win32

Type "help," "copyright," "credits," or "license" for more information.

>>>

Python is ready to use.

Install Python on Mac

Although the Mac already comes with Python installed, this is likely to be out of date and is only good for learning, not for developing. The best thing is to install a new version of Python and to do that; we need a C compiler.

Go to the Mac App store and download XCode.

Open a terminal and type in xcode-select –install—this will install the command line tools.

The next step is a package manager and the best one is called Homebrew and to install this, open a terminal and run the following code:

```
$       usrbin/ruby       -e       "$(curl       -fsSL
https://raw.githubusercontent.com/Homebrew/install/maste
r/install)"
```

Follow the on-screen instructions to install Homebrew and then prepare to make changes to the PATH environment variable. To do this, add this line at the bottom of the ~/.profile   file: export PATH=usrlocal/bin:usrlocal/sbin:$PATH.

Now you can install Python. For Python 2.7, type this is at the command:

```
$ brew install python
```

For Python 3, type this:

```
$ brew install python3
```

This will only take a couple of minutes at the most.

Homebrew will also install Pip and Setuptools. Setuptools lets you download and install Python software via a network, normally the Internet, using just a single command—easy_install. This will also let you add this capability for network installation to your Python software. Pip is used for the easy installation and management of Python packages and is recommended instead of using easy_install.

Chapter 4:

Using Python Shell IDLE and Writing Your First Program

Using Python Shell and IDLE

There are two ways to run a Python program, and that is using its runtime environment or using the command line interpreter. The command-line interpreter has two forms. The first one is the regular Python shell. The second one is IDLE or Integrated Development and Learning Environment. The regular Python shell uses the familiar command-line interface (CLI) or terminal look, while IDLE is a Python program encased in a regular graphical user interface (GUI) window. IDLE is full of the easy-to-access menu, customization options, and GUI functions, while the Python shell is devoid of those and only offers a command prompt (i.e., the input field in a text-based user interface screen).

One of the beneficial functions of IDLE is its syntax highlighting. The syntax highlighting function makes it easier for programmers or scripters to identify between keywords, operators, variables, and numeric literals.

Also, you can customize the highlight color and the font properties displayed on IDLE. With the shell, you only get a monospaced font, white font color, and black background.

All of the examples in this book are written in the Python shell. However, it is okay for you to write using IDLE. It is suited for beginners since they do not need to worry about indentation and code management. Not to mention that the syntax highlighting is truly beneficial.

Writing Your First Program

To get you started, code the below Hello World program. It has been a tradition for new programmers to start their learning with this simple program. Just write this line in the shell or IDLE and press Enter.

>>> print("Hello World!")

Hello World!

>>> _

Shell, IDLE, and Scripts Syntax

Prompt

The Python Shell and IDLE have a prompt, which looks like this: >>>. You generally start writing your code after the prompt in the Python Shell and IDLE. However, remember that when you write code in a file, py script, or module, you do not need to write the prompt.

For example:

Class thisClass():

def function1():

x = 1

print(x)

```
def function2():

pass
```

That is valid code.

Indentation

When programming, you will encounter or create code blocks. A code block is a piece of Python program text (or statement) that can be executed as a unit, such as a module, a class definition, or a function body.

They often end with a colon (:).

By default and by practice, indentation is done with four spaces. You can do away with any number of spaces as long as the code block has a uniform number of spaces before each statement.

For example:

```
def function1():

x = 1

print(x)

def function2():

y = "Sample Text"

print("Nothing to see here.")
```

That is a perfectly valid code. You can also use tab, but it is not recommended since it can be confusing, and you will get an error if you mix using tabs and spaces.

Also, if you change the number of spaces for every line of code, you will get an error. Here is an example in the shell.

Note the large space before print(x) on line 2.

>>> x = 1

>>> print(x)

File "<stdin>", line 1

print(x)

^

IndentationError: unexpected indent

>>> _

By the way, a statement is a line of code or instruction.

Indentation Prompt

When using the Python Shell, it will tell you when to indent by using the prompt (...). For example:

>>> def function1():

x = 1

print(x)

>>> def function2():

y = "Sample Text"

print("Nothing to see here.")

>>> _

In IDLE, an indentation will be **automatic**. And to escape an indentation or code block, you can just press Enter or go to the next line.

Python Shell Navigation

You cannot interact using a mouse with the Python Shell. Your mouse will be limited to the window's context menu, window commands such as minimize, maximize, and close, and scrolling.

Also, you can perform marking (selecting), copying, and pasting, but you need to use the windows context menu for that using the mouse. You can also change the appearance of the window and shell by going through the properties menu.

Most of the navigation you can do in the shell is moving the navigation caret (the blinking white underscore). You can move it using the navigation keys (left and right arrow keys, PgUp, PgDn, Home, End, etcetera). The up and down arrow keys' function is to browse through the previous lines you have written.

IDLE Navigation

The IDLE window is just like a regular GUI window. It contains a menu bar where you can access most of IDLE's functionalities. Also, you can use the mouse directly on IDLE's work area as if you are using a regular word processor.

You might need to take a quick look at the menu bar's function for you to familiarize yourself with them. Unlike the Python shell, IDLE provides a lot more helpful features that can help you with programming.

Primarily, IDLE is the main tool you can use to develop Python programs. However, you are not limited to it. You can use other development environments or word processors to create your scripts.

Troubleshooting Installation Issues

First of all, make sure that you download the installation file from the website: https://www.python.org. Next, make sure that you chose the proper installation file for your operating system. There are dedicated installation files for Windows, MacOSX, and other UNIX based operating system.

If your computer is running on Windows XP, the latest release of Python will not work on it. You must install and use Python 3.4. Also, remember that there are two versions of each release: a 32-bit and a 64-bit version. If you are unsure if your computer is running on 32 or 64-bit, then just get the 32-bit version. Normally, the recommended installer that the site will provide contains both and will detect which installer it will use automatically. Normally, you do not need to go to Python's website to download the installation file if you are using a Linux distribution as an operating system. You can just use your system's package manager.

Before installing Python, make sure that you have at least 100 MB free disk space. You can also edit the installation location of Python. However, take note of the location you type it if you wish to install Python in a different folder.

If the installer did not provide shortcuts for you, you can just create them. The Python shell is located in the root folder of your Python installation.

<Python installation folder>\python.exe

For example:

"C:\Python37\python.exe"

For IDLE, you can use its batch file located in:

<Python installation folder>\Lib\idlelib\idle.bat

For example:

"C:\Python37\Lib\idlelib\idle.bat"

If you cannot find the idlelib folder inside the Python Lib folder, reinstall Python and make sure that IDLE is checked.

Practice Exercise

For now, familiarize yourself with the Python shell and IDLE. Try to discover the things you can do with them. Look at all the messages that it may send you as you enter information on it.

When it comes to IDLE, try to customize it (e.g., change the color theme from the default IDLE Classic to IDLE Dark). Explore all the other features and functions you can change. Have fun!

Chapter 5:

The World of Variables and Operators

Operators

Python, just like with many programming languages, has numerous operators like arithmetic operators' addition (+), subtraction (-), multiplication (*), and division (/). Some of those operators have similar functionalities in most programming languages.

Operators are divided according to their functionality and the data type of expression or output that they produce.

Most operators use signs and symbols, while some use keywords. Some operators that perform uncommon or advanced data processing use functions.

Note that not adding space between operands and operators will work.

However, it is best that you avoid typing expressions like that to prevent any potential syntax errors.

Arithmetic Operators

Operation	Operator	Description	Example

Addition	+	Adds numbers.	>>> 1 + 1
			
			2
			
			>>> _

Subtraction	-	Subtracts numbers.	>>> 10 - 12
			
			-2
			
			>>> _

Multiplication	*	Multiplies numbers.	>>> 42 * 35
			
			1470
			
			>>> _

Division	/	Divides the left-hand number by the right-hand number.	>>> 132 / 11
			
			12
			
			>>> _

Floor Division	//	Divides the left-hand number by the right-hand number and returns only the whole number, effectively removing any decimal value from the	>>> 10 // 3
			
			3
			
			>>> _

		quotient.	

Modulus	%	Performs a floor division on the left-hand number by the right-hand number and returns the remainder.	>>> 133 / 11
			
			1
			
			>>> _

Exponent	**	Raises the left-hand number by the right-hand power.	>>> 4 ** 2
			
			16
			
			>>> _

Relational Operators

Operation	Operator	Description	Example

Is Equal to	==	Returns true if left and right-hand sides are equal.	>>> 999 == 999
			
			True
			
			>>> _

Is Not Equal to	!=	Returns true if left and right-hand sides are not equal.	>>> 24 != 123
			
			True
			
			>>> _

Is Greater Than	>	Returns true if the left-hand side's value is greater than the right-hand's side.	>>> 554 > 64
			
			True
			
			>>> _

Is Less Than	<	Returns true if the left-hand side's value is lesser than the right-hand's side.	>>> 16 < 664
			
			True
			
			>>> _

Is Equal or Greater Than	>=	Returns true if the left-hand side's value is greater or equal than the right-hand's side.	>>> 554 >= 64
			
			True
			
			>>> 554 >= 554
			
			True
			
			>>> _

Is Equal or Less Than	<=	Returns true if the left-hand side's value is lesser or equal than the right-hand's side.	>>> 16 <= 664
			
			True
			
			>>> 16 <= 16
			
			True
			
			>>> _

Assignment Operator

Operation	Operator	Description	Example

Assign	=	Assigns the value of the right-hand operand to the variable on the left.	>>> x = 1
			
			>>> x
			
			1
			
			>>> _

Add and Assign	+=	Adds the value of the left variable and the value of the right-hand operand and assign the result to the left variable.	>>> x = 14
			
			>>> x
			
			14
			
			>>> x += 16
			
			>>> x
			
			30
			
			>>> _

Subtract and Assign	-=	Subtracts the value of the left variable and the value of the right-hand operand and assign the result to the left variable.	>>> x = 30
			
			>>> x
			
			30
			
			>>> x -= 4
			
			>>> x
			
			26

			>>> _

Multiply and Assign	*=	Multiplies the value of the left variable and the value of the right-hand operand and assign the result to the left variable.	>>> x = 26
			
			>>> x
			
			26
			
			>>> x *= 10
			
			>>> x
			
			260
			
			>>> _

Divide and Assign	/=	Divides the value of the left variable by the value of the right-hand operand and assigns the result to the left variable.	>>> x = 260
			
			>>> x
			
			260
			
			>>> x /= 13
			
			>>> x
			
			20
			
			>>> _

Floor Divide and Assign	//=	Performs a floor division on the value of the left variable by the value of the right-hand operand and	>>> x = 20
			
			>>> x
			
			20
			
			>>> x //= 3

		assign the quotient as a whole number to the left variable.	>>> x
			
			6
			
			>>> _

Modulus and Assign	%=	Performs a floor division on the value of the left variable by the value of the right-hand operand and assign the remainder of the quotient to the left variable.	>>> x = 6
			
			>>> x
			
			6
			
			>>> x %= 4
			
			>>> x
			
			2
			
			>>> _

Exponent/Raise and Assign	%=	Raises the value of the left variable by the power of the value of the right-hand operand and assigns the result to the left variable.	>>> x = 2
			
			>>> x
			
			2
			
			>>> x **= 3
			
			>>> x
			
			8
			
			>>> _

Logical Operators

Operation	Operator	Description	Example

Logical And	and	Returns true if both of the operands are true.	>>> True and True
			
			 True
			
			 >>> _

Logical Or	or	Returns true if at least one of the operands is true.	>>> True or False
			
			 True
			
			 >>> _

Logical Not	NOT	Returns the negated logical state of the operand.	>>> not True
			
			 False
			
			 >>> _

Truth Table

The operator and will only return True if both of the operands are True. It will always return False otherwise.

The operator or will only return False if both operands are False.

Otherwise, it will always return True.

The operator **not** will return False if the operand is True and will return True if the operand is False.

Below are truth tables for operator 'and' and 'or.'

Left Operand	Logical Operator	Right Operand	Result
True		True	True
True		False	False
False	And	True	False
False		False	False

Left Operand	Logical Operator	Right Operand	Result
True		True	True
True		False	True
False	Or	True	True
False		False	False

Membership Operators

Operation	Operator	Description	Example

In	In	Returns True if the left operand's value is present in the value of the right operand.	>>> x = "cat and dog"
			
			>>> a = "cat"
			
			>>> b = "dog"
			
			>>> c =

			"mouse"
			>>> a in x
			True
			>>> b in x
			True
			>>> c in x
			False
			>>> _
Not In	not in	Returns true if the left operand's value is not present in the value of the right operand.	>>> x = "cat and dog"
			>>> a = "cat"
			>>> b = "dog"
			>>> c = "mouse"
			>>> a not in x
			False
			>>> b not in x
			False
			>>> c not in x
			True
			>>> _

Identity Operators

Operation	Operator	Description	Example

Is	is	Returns True if the left operand's identity is the same as the identity of the right operand.
		
		Note: It may appear that it returns True if the values of the operands are equal, but Python evaluates the identity or ID and not the values.
		
		Equal values of a single data or variable tend to receive similar IDs. Results of expressions may receive new IDs or overlap with existing IDs with similar values.
		
		To check the ID of variables and data, you need to use the id() keyword/function.
			>>> x = "a"
			
			>>> id(x)
			
			34232504
			
			>>> id("a")
			
			34232504
			
			>>> x is "a"
			
			True
			
			>>> x * 2
			
			'aa'
			
			>>> x * 2 is "aa"
			
			False
			
			>>> id(x * 2)
			
			39908384
			
			>>> id("aa")
			
			39908552
			
			>>> x * 2 is 2 * x
			
			False
			
			>>> id(x *

			2)

		If you want to compare if values of the operands are equal, use == operator instead.	39908552
			
			>>> id(2 * x)
			
			39908384
			
			>>> _

Is Not	is not	Returns True if the left operand's identity is not the same as the identity of the right operand.	>>> x = "a"
			
			>>> id(x)
			
			34232504
			
			>>> id("a")
			
			34232504
			
			>>> x is not "a"
			
			False
			
			>>> x * 2
			
			'aa'
			
			>>> x * 2 is not "aa"
			
			True
			
			>>> _

Bitwise Operators

Operation	Operator	Description	Example

Bitwise And (AND)	&	Returns 1 for bits if both operands have 1 on the same place value. Returns 0 for 0-0, 1-0, and 0-1 combinations.	>>> 0b1101 & 0b1001
			
			9
			
			>>> bin(9)
			
			'0b1001'
			
			>>> _

Bitwise Or (OR)	|	Returns 0 for bits if both operands have 0 on the same place value. Returns 1 for 1-1, 1-0, and 0-1 combinations.	>>> 0b1101 | 0b1001
			
			13
			
			>>> bin(13)
			
			'0b1101'
			
			>>> _

Bitwise Exclusive Or (XOR)	^	Returns 1 for bits if both operands have 0 and 1 on the same place value. Returns 0 for 1-1 and 0-0 combinations.	>>> 0b1101 ^ 0b1001
			
			4
			
			>>> bin(4)
			
			'0b100'
			
			>>> _

Bitwise	~	Flips each bit and	>>>

Complement		negates the value.	~0b1010
			-11
			>>> bin(-11)
			'-0b1011
			>>> _
Bitwise Left Shift	<<	Moves bits of the left operand to the left. The number of shifting of bits is according to the value of the right operand.	>>> 0b1010 << 2
			40
			>>> bin(40)
			'0b101000'
			>>> _
Bitwise Left Shift	>>	Moves bits of the left operand to the right. The number of shifting of bits is according to the value of the right operand.	>>> 0b1010 >> 2
			2
			>>> bin(2)
			'0b10'
			>>> _

Below are truth tables for operator 'and,' 'or,' and 'xor.'

Left Operand	Logical Operator	Right Operand	Result
1		1	1
1		0	0
0	&	1	0
0		0	0

Left Operand	Logical Operator	Right Operand	Result
1		1	1
1		0	1
0	|	1	1
0		0	0

Left Operand	Logical Operator	Right Operand	Result
1		1	0
1		0	1
0	^	1	1
0		0	0

Practice Exercise

Create code for the following scenarios.

Create 5 separate expressions that will lead to a result of 10025. You cannot use an arithmetic operator more than once and your first number must be 7.

The ages are 18, 21, 19, 52, 6, 33, 15, 46, 72, and 25.

Find the value of x using these details:

x = y + (a * b / c)

y = a + 151

b = c * (144 + y)

y = 10

c = 7

Johnny was born on February 14, 1967. How many days old was he on January 1, 2000?

A car was moving 20 miles per hour on a straight road. Every five minutes, it instantly decelerates by 5 miles per hour, keeps that speed for a minute and then instantly accelerates back to 20 miles per hour. How many miles will the car cover if it moves like that for an hour?

Variables

A software application consists of two fundamental parts: Logic and Data. Logic consists of the functionalities that are applied to data to accomplish a particular task. Application data can be stored in memory or hard disk. Files and databases are used to store data on hard disks. In memory, data is stored in the form of variables. Variable in programming is a memory location used to store some value. Whenever you store a value in a variable, that value is actually being stored at a physical location in memory. Variables can be thought of as a reference to a physical memory location. The size of the memory reserved for a variable depends on the type of value stored in the variable.

Creating a Variable

It is very easy to create a variable in Python. The assignment operator "=" is used for this purpose. The value to the left of the assignment operator is the variable identifier or name of the variable. The value to the right of the operator is the value assigned to the variable. Take a look at the following code snippet.

- Name = 'Mike' # A string variable.

- Age = 15 # An integer variable.

- Score = 102.5 # A floating type variable.

- Pass = True # A Boolean variable.

In the script above, we created four different types of variables. You can see that we did not specify the type of variable with the variable name. For instance, we did not write, "string Name" or "int Age." We only wrote the variable name. This is because Python is a loosely typed language. Depending upon the value being stored in a variable, Python assigns a type to the variable at runtime. For instance, when Python interpreter interprets the line "Age = 15," it checks the type of the value that is an integer in this case. Hence, Python understands that Age is an integer type variable.

To check a type of a variable, pass the variable name to "type" function, as shown below: type(Age).

You will see that the above script, when run, prints "int" in the output that is the type of age variables.

Python allows multiple an assignment that means that you can assign one value to multiple variables at the same time. Take a look at the following script: Age = Number = Point = 20 #Multiple Assignment:

print (Age)

print (Number)

print (Point)

In the script above, integer 20 is assigned to three variables: Age, Number, and Point. If you print the value of these three variables, you will see 20 thrice in the output. For any programming language, the basic part is to store the data in memory and process it. No matter what kind of operation we are going to perform, we must have the object of operation. It is difficult for a skilled woman to cook without rice. In Python language, constants and variables are the main ones. In fact, both of them are identification codes used by program designers to access data contents in memory.

The biggest difference between the two is that the contents of variables will change with the execution of the program, while the contents of constants are fixed forever. In the process of program execution, it is often necessary to store or use some data. For example, if you want to write a program to calculate the mid-term exam results, you must first input the students' results and then output the total score, average score, and ranking after calculation.

Variable Naming and Assignment

In a program, program statements or instructions tell the computer which data to access and execute step by step according to the instructions in the program statements. These data may be words or numbers. What we call variable is the most basic role in a programming language, that is, a named memory unit allocated by the compiler in programming to store changeable data contents. The computer will store it in "memory" and take it out for use when necessary. In order to facilitate identification, it must be given a name. We call such an object "variable." For example:

> > firstsample = 3

> > > second sample = 5

> > > result = firstsample + secondsample

In the above program statement, firstsample and secondsample resulting to be the variables, and number 3 is the variable value of firstsample. Since the capacity of memory is limited, in order to avoid wasting memory space, each variable will allocate memory space of different sizes according to requirements, so "Data Type" is used to regulate it.

Variable Declaration and Assignment

Python is an object-oriented language, all data are regarded as objects, and the method of an Object reference is also used in variable processing. The type of variable is determined when the initial value is given, so there is no need to declare the data type in advance. The value of a variable is assigned with "=" and beginners easily confuse the function of the assignment operator (=) with the function of "equal" in mathematics. In programming languages, the "=" sign is mainly used for assignment.

The syntax for declaring a variable is as follows:

Variable name = variable value

E.g. number = 10.

The above expression indicates that the value 10 is assigned to the variable number. In short, in Python language, the data type does not need to be declared in advance when using a variable, which is different from that in C language, which must be declared in advance before using a variable. Python interpretation and operation system will automatically determine the data type of the variable according to the value of the variable given or set. For example, the data type of the above variable number is an integer. If the content of the variable is a string, the data type of the variable is a string.

Variable Naming Rules

For an excellent programmer, the readability of program code is very important. Although variable names can be defined by themselves as long as they conform to Python's regulations, when there are more and more variables, simply taking variables with letter names such as abc will confuse people and greatly reduce readability. Considering the readability of the program, it is best to name it according to the functions and meanings are given by variables. For example, the variable that stores height is named "Height" and the variable that stores weight is named "Weight." Especially when the program scale is larger, meaningful variable names will become more important. For example, when declaring variables, in order to make the program readable, it is generally used to start with lowercase letters, such as score, salary, etc. In Python, variable names also need to conform to certain rules. If inappropriate names are used, errors may occur during program execution. Python is a case-sensitive language. In other words, number and Number are two different variables. Variable names are not limited in length. Variable names have the following limitations: the first character of a variable name must be an English letter, underlined "_" and cannot be a number. Subsequent characters can match other upper-and lowercase English letters, numbers, underlined "_," and no space character is allowed. You cannot use Python's built-in reserved words (or keywords). Although Python version 3. X supports foreign language variable names; it is recommended that you try not to use words to name variables. On the one hand, it is more troublesome to switch input methods when inputting program code. On the other hand, the reading of the program code will not be smooth. The so-called reserved word usually has a special meaning and function, so it will be reserved in advance and cannot be used as a variable name or any other identifier name. The following is an example of a valid variable name: pageresponse

fileName4563

level

Number_

dstance

The following is an example of an invalid variable name:

2_sample

for

$ levelone

The username learning classroom uses the help () function to query Python reserved word. The help () function is Python's built-in function. If you are not sure about the method and property usage of a specific object, you can use the help () function to query. The Python reserved words mentioned above can be viewed by using the help () function. As long as "help ()" is executed, the interactive help mode will be entered. In this mode, the instructions to be queried will be input, and the relevant instructions will be displayed. We can continue to input the instructions we want to query in help mode. When we want to exit the interactive help mode, we can input Q or quit. You can also take parameters when entering the help () command, such as help (" keywords "); Python will directly display help or description the information without entering interactive help mode.

Although Python uses dynamic data types, it is very strict in data processing, and its data type is "strong type." For example:

> > > firstsample = 5

> > > secondsample = "45"

> > > print (firstsample + secondsample) #

Shows that TypeError variable firstsample is of numeric type and variable secondsample is of string type.

Some programming languages will convert the type unconsciously and automatically convert the value A to the string type, so firstsample + secondsample will get 545. Python language prohibits different data types from operating, so executing the above statement obviously Indicates information about the wrong type.

There is a difference between "strongly typed" and "weakly typed" in the data types of strong and weak type programming languages in small classrooms. One of the trade-offs is the safety of data type conversion. The strong type has a strict inspection for data type conversion.

Different types of operations must be explicitly converted, and programs will not automatically convert. For example, Python and Ruby prefer strong types.

However, most weak type programming languages adopt Implicit Conversion. If you don't pay attention to it, unexpected type conversion will occur, which will lead to wrong execution results.

JavaScript is a weak type of programming language.

Static Type and Dynamic Type

When Python is executed, the way to determine the data type belongs to "dynamic type."

What Is the Dynamic Type?

The data types of programming languages can be divided into "Statically-Typed" and "Dynamically-Typed" according to the type checking method.

Static types are compiled with the type-checked first, so the variables must be explicitly declared before they are used. The types of variables cannot be arbitrarily changed during execution. Java and C are such programming languages. For example, the following C language program statement declares that the variable number is int integer type, and the initial value of the variable is set to 10. When we assign "apple" to number again, an error will occur because "apple" is a string, and compilation will fail due to type discrepancy during compilation.

int firstsample = 10

firstsample = "apple"

#Error:

Types Do Not Match

Dynamic types are compiled without prior type checking, and data types are determined according to variable values during execution. Therefore, there is no need to declare types before variables are used.

The same variable can also be given different types of values, and Python is a dynamic type. For example, the following program statement declares the variable number and sets the initial value to the integer 10. When we assign the string apple to number, the type will be automatically converted.

firstsample = 10

firstsample = "love"

Print (firstsample)

output string love

Python has a Garbage Collection mechanism. When the object is no longer in use, the interpreter will automatically recycle and free up memory space. In the above example, when the integer object number is reassigned to another string object, the original integer object will be deleted by the interpreter.

If the object is determined not to be used, we can also delete it by using the "del" command with the following syntax: del object name For example:

> > number = "apple"

> > > print(number) # output apple

> > > del number # deletes string object number

> > > print(number) #Error: number does not define the execution result.

Since the variable number has been deleted, if the number variable is used again, an undefined error message for the variable will appear.

Chapter 6:

Data Types in Python

Python supports different data types. Each variable should belong to one of the data types supported in Python. The data type determines the value that can be assigned to a variable, the type of operation that may be applied to the variable as well as the amount of space assigned to the variable.

Let us discuss different data types supported in Python.

Python Numbers

These data types help in the storage of numeric values. The creation of number-objects in Python is done after we have assigned a value to them. Consider the example given below:

total = 55

age = 26

The statement can be used for the deletion of single or multiple variables. This is shown below:

del total

del total, age

In the first statement, we are deleting a single variable; while in the second statement, we are deleting two variables. If the variables to be deleted are more than two, separate them with a comma and they will be deleted.

In Python, four numerical values are supported:

- Int.

- Float.

- Complex.

In Python 3, all integers are represented in the form of long integers.

The Python integer literals belong to the int class.

Example

Run the following statements consecutively on the Python interactive interpreter:

x=10

x

You can run it on the Python interactive interpreter, and you will observe the following:

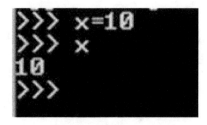

The float is used for storing numeric values with a decimal point.

Example

x=10.345

x

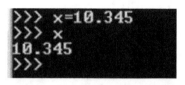

If you are performing an operation with one of the operands being a float and the other being an integer, the result will be a float.

Example

5 * 1.5

As shown above, the result of the operation is 7.5, which is a float.

Complex numbers are made of real and imaginary parts, with the imaginary part being denoted using a j. They can be defined as follows:

x = 4 + 5j

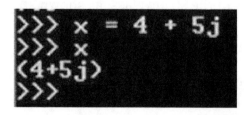

In the above example, 4 is the real part, while 5 is the imaginary part.

In Python, there is a function named type() that can determinate the type of a variable. You only have to pass the name of the variable inside that function as the argument and its type will be printed.

Example

x=10

type(x)

```
>>> x=10
>>> type(x)
<class 'int'>
>>>
```

The variable x is of int class, as shown above. You can try it for other variable types, as shown below:

name='nicholas'

type(name)

```
>>> name='nicholas'
>>> type(name)
<class 'str'>
>>>
```

The variable is of the string class, as shown above.

Python Strings

Python strings are a series of characters enclosed within quotes. Use any type of quotes to enclose Python strings, that is, single, double, or triple quotes. To access string elements, we use the slice operator. String characters begin at index 0, meaning that the first character string is at index 0. This is good when you need to access string characters. To concatenate strings in Python, we use + operator, the asterisk 9*) is used for repetition.

Example

#!usrbin/Python3

thanks = 'Thank You'

print (thanks) # to print the complete string

print (thanks[0]) # to print the first character of the string

print (thanks[2:7]) # to print the 3rd to the 7th character of the string

print (thanks[4:]) # to print from the 5th character of the string

print (thanks * 2) # to print the string two times

print (thanks + "\tAgain!") # to print a concatenated string

The program prints the following once executed:

```
Thank You
T
ank Y
k You
Thank YouThank You
Thank You        Again!
```

Notice that we have text beginning with the # symbol. The symbol denotes the beginning of a comment. The Python print will not act on the text from the symbol to the end of the line. Comments are meant to enhance the readability of code by giving explanations. We defined a string named *thanks* with the value *Thank You*. The *print (thanks[0])* statement helps us access the first character of the string; hence it prints T. You also notice that the space between the two words is counted as a character.

Python Tuples

In Python, Tuples are collections of data types that cannot be changed but can be arranged in a specific order. Tuples allow for duplicate items and are written within round brackets, as shown in the syntax below.

Tuple = ("string001", "string002", "string003")

print (Tuple)

Similar to the Python List, you can selectively display the desired string from a Tuple by referencing the position of that string inside a square bracket in the print command, as shown below.

Tuple = ("string001", "string002", "string003")

print (Tuple [1])

OUTPUT – ("string002")

The concept of *negative indexing* can also be applied to Python Tuple, as shown in the example below:

Tuple = ("string001", "string002", "string003", "string004", "string005")

print (Tuple [-2])

OUTPUT – ("string004")

You will also be able to specify a *range of indexes* by indicating the start and end of a range.

The result in values of such command on a Python Tuple would be a new Tuple containing only the indicated items, as shown in the example below:

Tuple = ("string001", "string002", "string003", "string004", "string005", "string006")

print (Tuple [1:5])

OUTPUT – ("string002", "string003", "string004", "string005")

Remember, the first item is at position 0 and the final position of the range, which is the fifth position in this example, is not included.

You can also specify a range of negative indexes to Python Tuples, as shown in the example below:

Tuple = ("string001", "string002", "string003", "string004", "string005", "string006")

print (Tuple [-4: -2])

OUTPUT – ("string004", "string005")

Remember, the last item is at position -1 and the final position of this range, which is the negative fourth position in this example, is not included in the Output.

Unlike Python lists, you cannot directly *change the data value of Python Tuples* after they have been created. However, conversion of a Tuple into a List and then modifying the data value of that List will allow you to create a Tuple subsequently from that updated List. Let's look at the example below:

Tuple1 = *("string001", "string002", "string003", "string004", "string005", "string006") List1 = list (Tuple1)*

List1 [2] = "update this list to create new tuple"

Tuple1 = tuple (List1)

print (Tuple1)

OUTPUT – ("string001", "string002", "update this list to create new tuple", "string004", "string005", "string006")

You can also determine the *length* of a Python Tuple using the "len()" function, as shown in the example below:

Tuple = ("string001", "string002", "string003", "string004", "string005", "string006")

print (len (Tuple))

OUTPUT – **6**

You cannot selectively delete items from a Tuple, but you can use the "del" keyword to *delete the Tuple* in its entirety, as shown in the example below:

Tuple = ("string001", "string002", "string003", "string004")

del Tuple

print (Tuple)

OUTPUT – name 'Tuple' is not defined

You can *join multiple Tuples* with the use of the "+" logical operator.

Tuple1 = ("string001", "string002", "string003", "string004")

Tuple2 = (100, 200, 300)

Tuple3 = Tuple1 + Tuple2

print (Tuple3)

OUTPUT – ("string001", "string002", "string003", "string004", 100, 200, 300)

You can also use the "tuple ( )" constructor to create a Tuple, as shown in the example below:

Tuple1 = tuple (("string001", "string002", "string003", "string004"))

print (Tuple1)

- **Exercise** – Create a Tuple "X" with string data values as "pies, cake, bread, scone, cookies" and display the item at -3 position.

Use Your Discretion Here And Write Your Code First

Now, check your code against the correct code below:

X = ("pies", "cake", "bread", "scone", "cookies")

print (X [-3])

OUTPUT – ("bread")

- **Exercise** – Create a Tuple "X" with string data values as "pies, cake, bread, scone, cookies" and display items ranging from -2 to -4.

Use Your Discretion Here And Write Your Code First

Now, check your code against the correct code below:

X = ("pies", "cake", "bread", "scone", "cookies")

print (X [-4 : -2])

OUTPUT – ("cake", "bread")

- **Exercise** – Create a Tuple "X" with string data values as "pies, cake, bread, scone, cookies" and change its item from "cookies" to "tart" using List function.

Use Your Discretion Here And Write Your Code First

Now, check your code against the correct code below:

X = ("pies", "cake", "bread", "scone", "cookies")

Y = list (X)

Y [4] = "tart"

X = tuple (Y)

print (X)

OUTPUT – ("pies", "cake", "bread", "scone", "tart")

- **Exercise** – Create a Tuple "X" with string data values as "pies, cake, cookies" and another Tuple "Y" with numeric data values as (2, 12, 22), then join them together.

Use Your Discretion Here And Write Your Code First

Now, check your code against the correct code below:

X = ("pies", "cake", "cookies")

Y = (2, 12, 22)

Z = X + Y

print (Z)

OUTPUT – ("pies", "cake", "cookies", 2, 12, 22)

Python Booleans

In the process of developing a software program, there is often a need to confirm and verify whether an expression is true or false. This is where Python Boolean data type and data values are used. In Python, comparing and evaluating two data values will result in one of the two Boolean values: "True" or "False."

Here are some examples of the comparison statement of numeric data leading to Boolean value:

print (100 > 90)

OUTPUT – True

print (100 == 90)

OUTPUT – False

print (100 < 90)

OUTPUT – False

Let's look at the **"bool ()"** function now, which allows for the evaluation of numeric data as well as string data resulting in "True" or "False" Boolean values.

print (bool (99))

OUTPUT - True

print (bool ("Welcome"))

OUTPUT - True

Here are some key points to remember for Booleans:

- If a statement has some kind of content, it would be evaluated as "True."

- All string data values will be resulting as "True" unless the string is empty.

- All numeric values will be resulting as "True" except "0."

- Lists, Tuples, Set, and Dictionaries will be resulting as "True" unless they are empty.

- Mostly empty values like (), [], {}, "", False, None and 0 will be resulting as "False."

- Any object created with the *"len"* function that results in the data value as "0" or "False" will be evaluated as "False."

In Python there are various built-in functions function that can be evaluated as Boolean, for example, the "isinstance()" function, which allows you to determine the data type of an object. Therefore, in order to check if an object is an integer, the code will be as below: $X = 123$

print (isinstance (X, int))

- **Exercise** – Create two variables "X" with string data values as "Just do it!" and "Y" with numeric data value as "3.24" and evaluate them.

Use Your Discretion Here And Write Your Code First

Now, check your code against the correct code below:

X = "Just do it!"

Y = 3.24

print (bool (X))

print (bool (Y))

OUTPUT –

True

True

Python Lists

In Python, lists are collections of data types that can be changed, organized, and include duplicate values. Lists are written within square brackets, as shown in the syntax below.

X = ["string001", "string002", "string003"]

print (X)

The same concept of position applies to Lists as the string data type, which dictates that the first string is considered at position 0. Subsequently, the strings that will follow are given positions 1, 2, and so on. You can selectively display the desired string from a List by referencing the position of that string inside a square bracket in the print command, as shown below.

X = ["string001", "string002", "string003"]

print (X [2])

OUTPUT – [string003]

Similarly, the concept of *negative indexing* is also applied to Python List. Let's look at the example below:

X = ["string001", "string002", "string003"]

print (X [-2])

OUTPUT – [string002]

You will also be able to specify a *range of indexes* by indicating the start and end of a range. The result in values of such command on a Python List would be a new List containing only the indicated items. Here is an example for your reference.

X = ["string001", "string002", "string003", "string004", "string005", "string006"]

print (X [2 : 4])

OUTPUT – ["string003", "string004"]

Remember, the first item is at position 0, and the final position of the range (4) is not included.

Now, if you do not indicate the start of this range, it will default to the position 0, as shown in the example below:

X = ["string001", "string002", "string003", "string004", "string005", "string006"]

print (X [: 3])

OUTPUT – ["string001", "string002", "string003"]

Similarly, if you do not indicate the end of this range, it will display all the items of the List from the indicated start range to the end of the List, as shown in the example below:

X = ["string001", "string002", "string003", "string004", "string005", "string006"]

print (X [3 :])

OUTPUT – ["string004", "string005", "string006"]

You can also specify a *range of negative indexes* to Python Lists, as shown in the example below:

X = ["string001", "string002", "string003", "string004", "string005", "string006"]

print (X [-3 : -1])

OUTPUT – ["string004", "string005"]

* Remember the last item is at position -1, and the final position of this range (-1) is not included in the Output.

There might be instances when you need to *change the data value* for a Python List.

This can be accomplished by referring to the index number of that item and declaring the new value.

Let's look at the example below:

X = ["string001", "string002", "string003", "string004", "string005", "string006"]

X [3] = "newstring"

print (X)

OUTPUT – ["string001", "string002", "string003", "newstring", "string005", "string006"]

You can also determine the *length* of a Python List using the "len()" function, as shown in the example below:

X = ["string001", "string002", "string003", "string004", "string005", "string006"]

print (len (X))

OUTPUT – 6

Python Lists can also be changed by *adding new items* to an existing list using the built-in "append ()" method, as shown in the example below:

X = ["string001", "string002", "string003", "string004"]

X.append ("newstring")

print (X)

OUTPUT – ["string001", "string002", "string003", "string004", "newstring"]

You can also, add a new item to an existing Python List at a specific position using the built-in "insert ()" method, as shown in the example below:

X = ["string001", "string002", "string003", "string004"]

X.insert (2, "newstring")

print (X)

OUTPUT – ["string001", "string002", "newstring", "string004"]

There might be instances when you need to *copy* an existing Python List. This can be accomplished by using the built-in "copy ( )" method or the "list ( )" method, as shown in the example below:

X = ["string001", "string002", "string003", "string004", "string005", "string006"]

Y = X.copy( )

print (Y)

OUTPUT   –   ["string001",   "string002",   "string003", "string004", "string005", "string006"]

X = ["string001", "string002", "string003", "string004", "string005", "string006"]

Y = list (X)

print (Y)

OUTPUT   –   ["string001",   "string002",   "string003", "string004", "string005", "string006"]

There are multiple built-in methods to *delete items* from a Python List.

- To selectively delete a specific item, the "remove ()" method can be used.

X = ["string001", "string002", "string003", "string004"]

X.remove ("string002")

print (X)

OUTPUT - ["string001", "string003", "string004"]

- To delete a specific item from the List, the "pop ()" method can be used with the position of the value. If no index has been indicated, the last item of the index will be removed.

X = ["string001", "string002", "string003", "string004"]

X.pop ( )

print (X)

OUTPUT - ["string001", "string002", "string003"]

- To delete a specific index from the List, the "del ()" method can be used, followed by the index within square brackets.

X = ["string001", "string002", "string003", "string004"]

del X [2]

print (X)

OUTPUT - ["string001", "string002", "string004"]

- To delete the entire List variable, the "del ()" method can be used, as shown below.

X = ["string001", "string002", "string003", "string004"]

del X

OUTPUT - .....

- To delete all the string values from the List without deleting the variable itself, the "clear ()" method can be used, as shown below.

X = ["string001", "string002", "string003", "string004"]

X.clear()

print (X)

OUTPUT – [ ]

Concatenation of Lists

You can join multiple lists with the use of the "+" logical operator or by adding all the items from one list to another using the "append ( )" method. The "extend ( )" method can be used to add a list at the end of another list. Let's look at the examples below to understand these commands.

X = ["string001", "string002", "string003", "string004"]

Y = [10, 20, 30, 40]

Z = X + Y

print (Z)

OUTPUT – ["string001", "string002", "string003", "string004", 10, 20, 30, 40]

X = ["string001", "string002", "string003", "string004"]

Y = [10, 20, 30, 40]

For x in Y:

X.append (x)

print (X)

OUTPUT – ["string001", "string002", "string003", "string004", 10, 20, 30, 40]

X = ["string001", "string002", "string003"]

Y = [10, 20, 30]

X.extend (Y)

print (X)

OUTPUT – ["string001", "string002", "string003", 10, 20, 30]

- **Exercise** – Create a list "A" with string data values as "red, olive, cyan, lilac, mustard" and display the item at -2 position.

Use Your Discretion Here And Write Your Code First

Now, check your code against the correct code below:

A = *[*"red", "olive", "cyan", "lilac", "mustard"]

print (A [-2])

OUTPUT – ["lilac"]

- **Exercise** – Create a list "A" with string data values as "red, olive, cyan, lilac, mustard" and display the items ranging from the string on the second position to the end of the string.

Use Your Discretion Here And Write Your Code First

Now, check your code against the correct code below:

A = ["red", "olive", "cyan", "lilac", "mustard"]

print (A [2 :])

OUTPUT – ["cyan", "lilac", "mustard"]

- **Exercise** – Create a list "A" with string data values as "red, olive, cyan, lilac, mustard" and replace the string "olive" with "teal."

Use Your Discretion Here And Write Your Code First

Now, check your code against the correct code below:

A = ["red", "olive", "cyan", "lilac", "mustard"]

A [1] = ["teal"]

print (A)

OUTPUT – ["red", "teal", "cyan", "lilac", "mustard"]

- **Exercise** – Create a list "A" with string data values as "red, olive, cyan, lilac, mustard" and copy the list "A" to create list "B."

Use Your Discretion Here And Write Your Code First

Now, check your code against the correct code below:

A = ["red", "olive", "cyan", "lilac", "mustard"]

B = A.copy ( )

print (B)

OUTPUT – ["red", "olive", "cyan", "lilac", "mustard"]

- **Exercise** – Create a list "A" with string data values as "red, olive, cyan, lilac, mustard" and delete the strings "red" and "lilac."

use your discretion here and write your code first

Now, check your code against the correct code below:

A = ["red", "olive", "cyan", "lilac", "mustard"]

del.A [0, 2]

print (A)

OUTPUT – ["olive", "cyan", "mustard"]

Python Sets

In Python, Sets are collections of data types that cannot be organized and indexed. Sets do not allow for duplicate items and must be written within curly brackets, as shown in the syntax below:

set = {"string1", "string2", "string3"}

print (set)

Unlike the Python List and Tuple, you cannot selectively display desired items from a Set by referencing the position of that item because the Python Set are not arranged in any order. Therefore, items do not have any indexing. However, the "for" loop can be used on Sets (more on this topic later in this chapter). Unlike Python Lists, you cannot directly *change the data values of Python Sets* after they have been created. However, you can use the "add ()" method to add a single item to Set and use the "update ( )" method to one or more items to an already existing Set. Let's look at the example below:

set = {"string1", "string2", "string3"}

set. add ("newstring")

print (set)

OUTPUT – {"string1", "string2", "string3", "newstring"}

set = {"string1", "string2", "string3"}

set. update (["newstring1", "newstring2", "newstring3",)

print (set)

OUTPUT – {"string1", "string2", "string3", "newstring1", "newstring2", "newstring3"}

You can also determine the *length* of a Python Set using the "len()" function, as shown in the example below:

set = {"string1", "string2", "string3", "string4", "string5", "string6", "string7"}

print (len(set))

OUTPUT – 7

To *delete a specific item from a Set*, the "remove ()" method can be used as shown in the code below:

set = {"string1", "string2", "string3", "string4", "string5"}

set. remove ("string4")

print (set)

OUTPUT – {"string1", "string2", "string3", **"string5"**}

You can also use the "discard ( )" method to delete specific items from a Set, as shown in the example below:

set = {"string1", "string2", "string3", "string4", "string5"}

set. discard ("string3")

print (set)

OUTPUT – {"string1", "string2", "string4", **"string5"**}

The "pop ( )" method can be used to delete only the last item of a Set.

It must be noted here that since the Python Sets are unordered, any item that the system deems as the last item will be removed.

 As a result, the output of this method will be the item that has been removed.

set = {"string1", "string2", "string3", "string4", "string5"}

A = set.pop ( )

print (A)

print (set)

OUTPUT –

String2

{"string1", "string3", "string4", *"string5"*}

To delete the entire Set, the "del" keyword can be used, as shown below.

set = {"string1", "string2", "string3", "string4", "string5"}

delete set

print (set)

OUTPUT – name 'set' is not defined

To delete all the items from the Set without deleting the variable itself, the "clear ()" method can be used, as shown below:

set = {"string1", "string2", "string3", "string4", "string5"}

set.clear ( )

print (set)

OUTPUT – set ( )

You can *join multiple Sets* with the use of the "union ( )" method. The output of this method will be a new set that contains all items from both the sets. You can also use the "update ( )" method to insert all the items from one set into another without creating a new Set.

Set1 = {"string1", "string2", "string3", "string4", "string5"}

Set2 = {15, 25, 35, 45, 55}

Set3 = Set1.union (Set2)

print (Set3)

OUTPUT – {"string1", 15, "string2", 25, "string3", 35, "string4", 45, "string5", 55}

Set1 = {"string1", "string2", "string3", "string4", "string5"}

Set2 = {15, 25, 35, 45, 55}

Set1.update (Set2)

print (Set1)

OUTPUT – {25, "string1", 15, "string4",55, "string2", 35, "string3", 45, "string5"}

You can also use the "set ( )" constructor to create a Set, as shown in the example below:

Set1 = set (("string1", "string2", "string3", "string4", "string5"))

print (Set1)

OUTPUT – {"string3", "string5", "string2", "string4", "string1"}

- **Exercise** – Create a Set "Veg" with string data values as "pies, cake, bread, scone, cookies" and add new items "tart," "custard," and "waffles" to this Set.

Use Your Discretion Here And Write Your Code First

Now, check your code against the correct code below:

Veg = {"pies", "cake", "bread", "scone", "cookies"}

Veg.update (["tart", "custard", "waffles"])

print (Veg)

OUTPUT – {"pies", "custard", "scone", "cake", "bread", "waffles", "cookies", "tart"}

- **Exercise** – Create a Set "Veg" with string data values as "pies, cake, bread, scone, cookies," then delete the last item from this Set.

Use Your Discretion Here And Write Your Code First

Now, check your code against the correct code below:

Veg = {"pies", "cake", "bread", "scone", "cookies"}

X = Veg.pop ( )

print (X)

print (Veg)

OUTPUT –

bread

{"pies", "scone", "cake", "cookies"}

- **Exercise** – Create a Set "Veg" with string data values as "pies, cake, bread, scone, cookies" and another Set "Veg2" with items as "tart, eggos, custard, waffles." Then combine both these Sets to create a third new Set.

Use Your Discretion Here And Write Your Code First

Now, check your code against the correct code below:

Veg = {"pies", "cake", "bread", "scone", "cookies"}

Veg2 = {"tart", "eggos", "custard", "waffles"}

AllVeg = Veg.union (Veg2) #this Set name may vary as it has not been defined in the exercise

print (AllVeg)

OUTPUT – {"pies", "custard", "scone", "cake", "eggos", "bread", "waffles", "cookies", "tart"}

Functions

This language consists of a number of built-in functions to use the integers while programming and can be used on any type of data. The Python standard library has the number of modules and to use the functions associated with these modules; you have to import the modules. Example: how to call a function *function_name (parameters)* e) *Lists*-also called as 'arrays' in every other programming language helps in grouping various types of data together. One can access the elements from the list, either at the beginning or at the end.

Example: coding a list, recalling and adding **cats = ['Tom', 'Snappy', 'Jessie', 'Kitty']**

print cats [2]

cats.append ('Catherine')

Dictionaries

These are unordered associative arrays that can be implemented using hash tables.

Example: how to create, add and delete entries in dictionary **#make phone book: Phonebook = {'Peter John':7766335, **

'Emily Johnson':99884444, 'Raja Ryan' : 7766544, \

'Jayati Mishra' : 88866655}

add the person 'Gagan Paul' to the phonebook: Phonebook ['Gagan Paul'] = 99886655

del phonebook ['Jayati Mishra']

Chapter 7:

Making Your Program Interactive

Learning the Python Interactive Developer Environment (IDE)

The best IDE to use with Python is Eclipse so, if it is already on your computer, you can skip ahead. If not, you need to install it and for that, you need Java runtime. Java tends to be pre-installed on most computers and to check if it is on yours, go to the command prompt and type in java -version.

If you haven't got Java, go to http://www.oracle.com/technetwork/java/javase/dpwnlads/index.html and download the latest version of Java. To install Eclipse:

Go to http://www.eclips..org/downloads and download the Eclipse installation. It will be in zip file format.

Unzip the file and that is it, nothing else to do; Eclipse will be installed on your system. To start Eclipse, go to the directory where you unzipped the file and double-click on eclipse.exe.

The Eclipse Python Plugin

PyDev is an Eclipse Python IDE and it can be used in several different Python distributions. It supports graphical debugging, code refactoring, code analysis, and lots more besides. PyDev can be installed through the Eclipse update manager by going to http://pydev.org/updates. Just check the box beside PyDev and follow the onscreen instructions to install it.

- Next, you need to configure Eclipse because it needs to know where Python is.

- Open Window>Preferences.

- Click on the option for PyDev and then click on Interpreter Python.

- Click New Configuration.

- Add the executable path for Python.

Eclipse IDE is now set up on your computer and ready to use with Python.

Learning the Python IDE

IDLE is the integrated development environment for Python and it is installed automatically with Python. As well as a neat graphical user interface, IDLE is packed with features that make using Python for developing easy, including a very powerful feature, syntax highlighting.

With syntax highlighting, reserved keywords, literal text, comments, etc. are all highlighted in different colors, making it much easier to see errors in your code. As well as editing your Python program with IDLE, you can also execute your programs in IDLE.

How to Write a Python Program and Run It in IDLE

- Start IDLE—open Start>All Programs>Python>IDLE.

- A window with a title of Python Shell will open.

- Click on File>New Window.

- Now a new window called Untitled will load.

- Click on File>Save As and choose a location for your program file.

- Where it says File Name, type program1/py in the box.

- Click on Save.

A blank window will open—this is an editor window and it is ready for you to type your program in.

Type the following statement in exactly as written—it will work on Python 2.x or 3.x:

print ("Hello World")

Open the Run menu and click on Run Module to run the program.

You will now see a message asking you to save your program (it will say Source) so click OK.

Your program will now run in a Python Shell window.

To quit Python, shut down all Python windows.

Important Note

If you want to open your file again, find it in the folder you saved it in. Right-click on it and then choose Edit with IDLE from the menu—this will open the editor window.

Chapter 8:

Making Choices and Decision

D ecisions are a core part of programming because we will always create programs that anticipate certain conditions to be met during normal execution.

As programmers, we must specify actions that the program should take when the conditions are met.

What decision structures do is to evaluate one or multiple expressions that return *TRUE* or *FALSE* outcomes.

We can then determine what actions the program should take by defining the statements to execute when the outcome is *TRUE* or *FALSE*.

The if statement

The diagram below is a flowchart diagram of a basic decision-making structure used in most programming languages.

In Python, any *non-null* and *non-zero* value returned is regarded as *TRUE* while a *null* or *zero* value is assumed to be *FALSE*.

The decision-making structure demonstrated in the figure above represents the most basic conditional statement that uses the *if* statement that we first used in Exercise8.py.

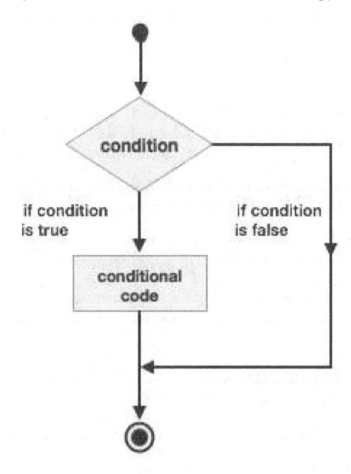

Here is the syntax of the *if* decision-making structure:

```
if condition_test:

statement
```

Note: Indentation is very important.

Exercise34: if statement.

```
x = 10

if x == 10:

 print ("x = 10")
```

What this simple exercise does is this:

First, the variable x is created and assigned a value of 10.

The decision-making structure if evaluates whether the value of x is equal to 10.

The string "x = 10" is displayed on the screen should the *if* statement evaluates TRUE.

Note that we can also write the *if* statement in this format:

```
x = 10

if x == 10: print ("x = 10")
```

The if... Else Statement

So far, we have seen that we can use the *if* statement to evaluate a condition and execute a statement when the results evaluate to TRUE. However, with the *if* statement, nothing happens when the condition evaluates to FALSE.

With the *if... else* statement, we can provide an alternative statement for the interpreter to execute should the condition being evaluated evaluate to FALSE.

Here is the flowchart diagram of the if... else structure of decision-making in Python:

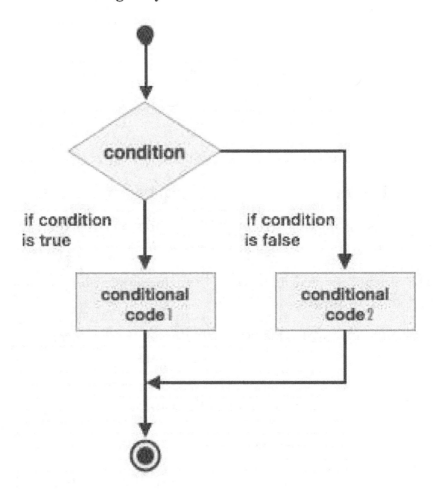

The syntax of an *if... else* statement takes this format:

```
if condition_test:

    statement_of_if

else:

    statement_of_else
```

Exercise35: if... else condition.

```
x, y = 12, 12


if (x == y ):

 print ("x is equal to y")

else:

 print ("x is not equal to y")
```

Can you change the values of the variables x or y to make them equal and see what happens when you run the script?

If...elif...else Statement

The *if... else* statement is a way for the program to evaluate a condition and execute a statement when the condition returns TRUE or executes another when it returns FALSE.

With Python, you can evaluate a condition more than once and use the *if... else* statement more than once.

However, rather than use an *else... if* statement, you can easily use elif. *elif* is the short of *else if*.

This is best demonstrated in Exercise36.py.

Exercise36.py: Nested if statements.

```
age = int(input("Enter age to evaluate:"))


if age >= 18:

 agegroup = "Adult"


elif age >= 13:

 agegroup = "Teenager"


elif age >=0:

 agegroup = "Child"


else:

 agegroup = "Invalid"


print (agegroup)
```

In Exercise36, the program prompts the user to enter an integer to evaluate. It checks whether the input is equal to or greater than 18 and, if *TRUE*, determines that the agegroup is

Adult. If it is not equal or greater than 18, which means the condition returns *FALSE*, it moves on to the next elif block for evaluation and so on. In the end, there is an else statement that is executed should all the elif statements return *FALSE*.

The flowchart diagram of the *if... elif... else* construct looks like this:

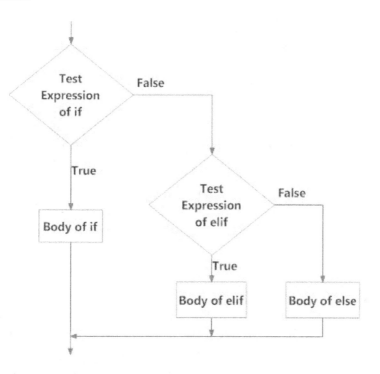

Nested if Statement

With Python, you can use one *if* or *if... elif... else* statement inside another *if... elif... else* statement or statements. This forms a nested structure of *if* and *if... else*'s. The only way to figure out which level of nesting a statement is before arriving at the last else statement is by using indentation. Because nesting if statements can be very confusing, you should try to avoid using it if you can.

Exercise37 illustrates how a nested if... elif... else statement looks like.

Exercise37: Nested if statement

```
number = float(input("Enter a
number to evaluate: "))

if number >= 0:

 if number == 0:

 print (number, "is a Zero")

 else:

 print (number, "is a positive
number")

else:

 print (number, "is a negative
number")
```

Decision-Making

Decision-making structures are common programming features. They are necessary for situations when a course of action may only be implemented if a test condition is satisfied. Decision-making constructs start with a Boolean expression that is either True or False. The program branches depending on the response to the expression. Python supports the following conditional statements:

- If statements

- If else statements

- If...elif...else statements

If Statements

An if statement starts with a Boolean expression, which is followed by statements specifying the action to be implemented if the response is True.

syntax:

if expression:

statement(s)

Example:

age = int(input("Enter your age: "))

if age >= 15:

print("Welcome to the Gamers Club!")

print("We only accept members from age 15 and up.")

Assuming you enter 18 as your age when you run the program:

Enter your age: 18

Welcome to the Gamers Club!

We only accept members from age 15 and up.

If you type 12, here's what the output would be:

Enter your age: 12

We only accept members from age 15 and up.

If...Else Statements

An if...else statement first evaluates the test expression. If the response to the test condition is True, it executes the statement in the 'if block.' If the response is False, it executes the statements in the 'else block.'

syntax:

if test condition:

statement(s)

else:

statement(s)

Example:

#this program checks if the store has a specific sports shoes brand on stock:

shoes = ["Nike", "Adidas", "Converse", "Reebok", "Puma"]

order = input("Please enter a brand: ")

if order in shoes:

print("We have it on stock!")

else:

print("Sorry, but " + order + " is out of stock.")

Run the program and type the brand Converse when prompted:

Please enter a brand: Converse

We have it on stock!

Run the program again and type another shoe brand, Fila:

Please enter a brand: Fila

Sorry, but Fila is out of stock.

If...Elif...if Statements

An if..elif...if statement uses an elif or 'else if' block, facilitating the evaluation of multiple expressions. The program first checks if the 'if expression' is True or False. If False, it evaluates the condition in the elif expression. If the elif expression is True, it executes the statement block under the elif expression. If False, the program executes the 'else block.'

syntax:

if test condition:

if block

elif test condition:

elif block

else:

else block

Example:

#this program checks if a shoe brand is on stock

#if not on stock, program will check if it's on order and prints appropriate remark

```
#if the brand is neither on stock or on order, program prints corresponding comment
on_stock = ["Nike", "Adidas", "Converse", "Reebok", "Puma"]
on_order = ["K-Swiss", "New Balance", "Asics", "Saucony", "Jordan"]
order = input("Please enter a brand: ")
if order in on_stock:
print("Great, we have it on stock!")
elif order in on_order:
print ("Your chosen brand " + order + " will be delivered within the week.")
else:
print("Sorry, " + order + " is currently out of stock.")
```

To test the above if...elif...else code, run the program and enter Nike when prompted for brand:

Please enter a brand: Nike

Great, we have it on stock!

Run it again and enter Jordan:

Please enter a brand: Jordan

Your chosen brand Jordan will be delivered within the week.

Run the program once more and this time enter Skechers:

Please enter a brand: Skechers

Sorry, Skechers is currently out of stock.

Chapter 9:

Functions and Modules

When you are working with a language like Python, there will be times when you will need to work with something that is known as a function.

These functions are going to be blocks of reusable code that you will use in order to get your specific tasks done.

But when you define one of these functions in Python, we need to have a good idea of the two main types of functions that can be used and how each of them works.

The two types of functions that are available here are known as built-in and user-defined.

The built-in functions are the ones that will come automatically with some of the packages and libraries that are available in Python.

Still, we are going to spend our time working with the user-defined functions because these are the ones that the developer will create and use for special codes they write.

In Python though, one thing to remember no matter what kind of function you are working with is that all of them will be treated like objects.

This is good news because it can make it a lot easier to work with these functions compared to what we may see with some other coding languages.

Built-in Functions				
abs()	divmod()	input()	open()	staticmethod()
all()	enumerate()	int()	ord()	str()
any()	eval()	isinstance()	pow()	sum()
basestring()	execfile()	issubclass()	print()	super()
bin()	file()	iter()	property()	tuple()
bool()	filter()	len()	range()	type()
bytearray()	float()	list()	raw_input()	unichr()
callable()	format()	locals()	reduce()	unicode()
chr()	frozenset()	long()	reload()	vars()
classmethod()	getattr()	map()	repr()	xrange()
cmp()	globals()	max()	reversed()	zip()
compile()	hasattr()	memoryview()	round()	__import__()
complex()	hash()	min()	set()	
delattr()	help()	next()	setattr()	
dict()	hex()	object()	slice()	
dir()	id()	oct()	sorted()	

The user-defined functions that we are going to talk about in the next section are going to be important and can really expand out some of the work that we are doing as well. But we also need to take a look at some of the work that we are able to do with our built-in functions as well. The list above includes many of the ones that are found inside of the Python language. Take some time to study them and see what they are able to do to help us get things done.

Why Are User-Defined Functions So Important?

- To keep it simple, a developer is going to have the option of either writing out some of their own functions, known as a user-defined function, or they are able to go through and borrow a function from another library, one that may not be directly associated with Python. These functions are sometimes going to provide us with a few advantages depending on how and when we would like to use them in the code. Some things to remember when working on these user-defined functions and to gain a better understanding of how they work will be the functions that will be made with code blocks that are reusable. It is necessary to write them out once and then you can use them as many times as you need in the code. You can even take that user-defined function and use it in some of your other applications as well.

- These functions can also be very useful. You can use them to help with anything you want, from writing out specific logic in business to working on common utilities. You can also modify them based on your own requirements to make the program work properly.

- The code is often going to be friendly for developers, easy to maintain, and well-organized all at once. This means that you are able to support the approach for modular design.

You are able to write out these types of functions independently, and the tasks of your project can be distributed for rapid application development if needed. A user-defined function that is thoughtfully and well-defined can help ease the process for the development of an application. Now that we know a little bit more about the basics of a user-defined function, it is time to look at some of the different arguments that can come with these functions before moving on to some of the codes you can use with this kind of function.

Options for Function Arguments

Any time you are ready to work with these kinds of functions in your code, you will find that they have the ability to work with four types of arguments. These arguments and the meanings behind them are something that will be pre-defined, and the developer is not always going to be able to change them up. Instead, the developer is going to have the option to use them but follow the rules that are there with them. You do get the option to add a bit to the rules to make the functions work the way that you want. As we said before, there are four argument types you can work with and these include:

- **Default arguments:** In Python, we are going to find that there is a bit different way to represent the default values and the syntax for the arguments of your functions. These default values are going to be the part that indicates that the argument of the function is going to take that value if you don't have a value for the argument that can pass through the call of the function. The best way to figure out where the default value is will be to look for the equal sign.

- **Required argument:** The next type of argument is going to be the required arguments. Some kinds of arguments will be mandatory to the function that you are working on. These values need to go through and be passed in the right order and number when the function is called out, or the code won't be able to run the right way.

- **Keyword arguments:** These are going to be the argument that will be able to help with the function call inside of Python. These keywords are going to be the ones that we mention through the function call, along with some of the values that will go all through this one. These keywords will be mapped with the function argument so that you are able to identify all of the values, even if you don't keep the same order when the code is called.

- **Variable arguments:** The last argument that we are going to take a look at here is the variable number of arguments. This is good for working when you are not sure how many arguments are going to be necessary for the code that you are writing to pass the function. Or you can use this to design your code where any number of arguments can be passed, as long as they have been able to pass any of the requirements in the code that you set.

Writing a Function

Now that we have a little better idea of what these functions are like and some of the argument types that are available in Python, it is time for us to learn the steps you need to accomplish all of this.

There are going to be four basic steps that we are able to use to make all of this happen, and it is really up to the programmer how difficult or simple you would like this to be. We will start with some of the basics, and then you can go through and make some adjustments as needed. Some of the steps that we need to take in order to write out our own user-defined functions include:

- **Declare your function.** You will need to use the "def" keyword and then have the name of the function come right after it.

- **Write out the arguments.** These need to be inside the two parentheses of the function. End this declaration with a colon to keep up with the proper writing protocol in this language.

- Add in the statements that the program is supposed to execute at this time.

- **End the function.** You can choose whether you would like to do it with a return statement or not.

An example of the syntax that you would use when you want to make one of your own user-defined functions includes:

def userDefFunction (arg1, arg2, arg3, ...):

program statement1

program statement2

program statement3

....

Return;

Working with functions can be a great way to ensure that your code is going to behave the way you would like. Making sure that you get it set up in the proper manner and that you are able to work through these functions, getting them set up in the manner that you would like, can be really important as well. There are many times when the functions will come out and serve some purpose, so taking the time now to learn how to use them can be very important to the success of your code.

Python Modules

Modules consist of definitions as well as program statements. An illustration is a file name config.py that is considered as a module. The module name would be config. Modules are sued to help break large programs into smaller manageable and organized files as well as promoting reusability of code.

Example

Creating the First module

Def add(x, y):

"""This is a program to add two numbers and return the outcome"""

outcome=x+y

return outcome

Module Import

The keyword import is used to import.

Example

Import first

The dot operator can help us access a function as long as we know the name of the module.

Example

Start IDLE.

Navigate to the File menu and click New Window.

Type the following:

first.add(6,8)

Import Statement in Python

The import statement can be used to access the definitions within a module via the dot operator.

Start IDLE.

Navigate to the File menu and click New Window.

Type the following:

import math

print("The PI value is", math.pi) Import with renaming

Example

Start IDLE.

Navigate to the File menu and click New Window.

Type the following:

import math as h

print("The PI value is-",h.pi)

Explanation

In this case, h is our renamed math module with a view helping save typing time in some instances. When we rename, the new name becomes a valid and recognized one and not the original one.

From...import statement Python.

It is possible to import particular names from a module rather than importing the entire module.

Example

Start IDLE.

Navigate to the File menu and click New Window.

Type the following:

from math import pi

print("The PI value is-", pi)

Importing All Names

Example

Start IDLE.

Navigate to the File menu and click New Window.

Type the following:

from math import*

print("The PI value is-", pi)

Explanation

In this context, we are importing all definitions from a particular module, but it is an encouraged norm as it can lead to unseen duplicates.

Module Search Path in Python

Example

Start IDLE.

Navigate to the File menu and click New Window.

Type the following:

import sys

sys.path

Python searches everywhere, including the sys file.

Reloading a Module

Python will only import a module once, increasing efficiency in execution.

print("This program was executed") import mine

Reloading Code

Example

Start IDLE.

Navigate to the File menu and click New Window.

Type the following:

import mine

import mine

import mine

mine.reload(mine)

Dir() built-in Python function

For discovering names contained in a module, we use the dir() inbuilt function.

Syntax

dir(module_name)

Python Package

Files in python hold modules and directories are stored in packages. A single package in Python holds similar modules. Therefore, different modules should be placed in different Python packages.

Chapter 10:

Working with Files

Programs are made with input and output in mind. You input data to the program, the program processes the input and it ultimately provides you with an output.

For example, a calculator will take in numbers and operations you want. It will then process the operation you wanted, and then it will display the result to you as its output.

There are multiple ways for a program to receive input and to produce output. One of those ways is to read and write data on files.

To start learning how to work with files, you need to learn the open() function.

The open() function has one **required** parameter and two **optional** parameters. The first and required parameter is the file name.

The second parameter is the access mode, and the third parameter is buffering or buffer size. The file name parameter requires string data.

The access mode requires string data, but there is a set of string values you can use and is defaulted to "r." The buffer size parameter requires an integer and is defaulted to 0. To practice using the open() function, create a file with the name sampleFile.txt inside your Python directory.

Try this sample code:

```
>>> file1 = open("sampleFile.txt")

>>> _
```

Note that the file function returns a file object. The statement in the example assigns the file object to variable file1.

The file object has multiple attributes, and three of them are:

- **Name:** This contains the name of the file.

- **Mode:** This contains the access mode you used to access the file.

- **Closed:** This returns False if the file has been opened and True if the file is closed. When you use the open() function, the file is set to open.

Now, access those attributes.

```
>>> file1 = open("sampleFile.txt")

>>> file1.name

'sampleFile.txt'

>>> file1.mode

'r'

>>> file1.closed

False

>>> _
```

Whenever you are finished with a file, close them using the close() method.

```
>>> file1 = open("sampleFile.txt")
```

```
>>> file1.closed
```

False

```
>>> file1.close()
```

```
>>> file1.closed
```

True

```
>>> _
```

Remember that closing the file does not delete the variable or object. To reopen the file, just open and reassign the file object. For example:

```
>>> file1 = open("sampleFile.txt")
```

```
>>> file1.close()
```

```
>>> file1 = open(file1.name)
```

```
>>> file1.closed
```

False

```
>>> _
```

Reading from a File

Before proceeding, open the sampleFile.txt in your text editor. Type "Hello World" in it and save. Go back to Python.

To read the contents of the file, use the read() method. For example:

```
>>> file1 = open("sampleFile.txt")
```

```
>>> file1.read()
```

'Hello World'

```
>>> _
```

File Pointer

Whenever you access a file, Python sets the file pointer. The file pointer is like your word processor's cursor. Any operation on the file starts at where the file pointer is. When you open a file and when it is set to the default access mode, which is "r" (read-only), the file pointer is set at the beginning of the file. To know the current position of the file pointer, you can use the tell() method. For example: >>> file1 = open("sampleFile.txt")

```
>>> file1.tell()
```

0

```
>>> _
```

Most of the actions you perform on the file move the file pointer. For example:

```
>>> file1 = open("sampleFile.txt")
```

```
>>> file1.tell()
```

0

```
>>> file1.read()
```

'Hello World'

```
>>> file1.tell()
```

11

```
>>> file1.read()
```

"

```
>>> _
```

To move the file pointer to a position you desire, you can use the seek() function. For example:

```
>>> file1 = open("sampleFile.txt")
```

```
>>> file1.tell()
```

0

```
>>> file1.read()
```

'Hello World'

```
>>> file1.tell()
```

11

```
>>> file1.seek(0)
```

0

```
>>> file1.read()
```

'Hello World'

```
>>> file1.seek(1)
```

1

```
>>> file1.read()
```

'ello World'

```
>>> _
```

The seek() method has two parameters. The first is offset, which sets the pointer's position depending on the second parameter. Also, an argument for this parameter is required.

The second parameter is optional. It is for whence, which dictates where the "seek" will start. It is set to 0 by default.

If set to 0, Python will set the pointer's position to the offset argument. If set to 1, Python will set the pointer's position relative or in addition to the current position of the pointer.

If set to 2, Python will set the pointer's position relative or in addition to the file's end.

Note that the last two options require the access mode to have binary access. If the access mode does not have binary access, the last two options will be useful to determine the current position of the pointer [seek(0, 1)] and the position at the end of the file [seek(0, 2)]. For example: >>> file1 = open("sampleFile.txt")

>>> file1.tell()

0

>>> file1.seek(1)

1

>>> file1.seek(0, 1)

0

>>> file1.seek(0, 2)

11

>>> _

File Access Modes

To write to a file, you will need to know more about file access modes in Python. There are three types of file operations: reading, writing, and appending.

Reading allows you to access and copy any part of the file's content. Writing allows you to overwrite a file's contents and create a new one. Appending allows you to write on the file while keeping the other content intact.

There are two types of file access modes: string and binary. String access allows you to access a file's content as if you are opening a text file. Binary access allows you to access a file in its rawest form: binary.

In your sample file, accessing it using string access allows you to read the line "Hello World." Accessing the file using binary access will let you read "Hello World" in binary, which will be b'Hello World'. For example: >>> x = open("sampleFile.txt", "rb")

>>> x.read()

b'Hello World'

>>> _

String access is useful for editing text files. Binary access is useful for anything else, like pictures, compressed files, and executables. In this book, you will only be taught how to handle text files.

There are multiple values that you can enter in the file access mode parameter of the open() function, but you do not need to memorize the combination. You just need to know the letter combinations.

Each letter and symbol stand for an access mode and operation.

For example:

r = read only—file pointer placed at the beginning

r+ = read and write

a = append—file pointer placed at the end

a+ = read and append

w = overwrite/create—file pointer set to 0 since you create the file

w+ = read and overwrite/create

b = binary

By default, file access mode is set to string. You need to add b to allow binary access. For example: "rb."

Writing to a File

When writing to a file, you must always remember that Python overwrites and not insert file. **For example:**

>>> x = open("sampleFile.txt", "r+")

>>> x.read()

'Hello World'

>>> x.tell(0)

0

>>> x.write("text")

4

```
>>> x.tell()
```

4

```
>>> x.read()
```

'o World'

```
>>> x.seek(0)
```

0

```
>>> x.read()
```

'texto World'

```
>>> _
```

You might have expected that the resulting text will be "textHello World." The write method of the file object replaces each character one by one, starting from the current position of the pointer.

Using Files

Like for other high-level languages, files are another useful concept that Python supports. Apart from reading input from files and writing output to files, Python offers some useful hacks to work with files and directories that can be very handy when trying to write automated scripts on the file systems.

To open/create a file

Sample Code

```
>>>>f = open("file1.txt") #returns a file object
```

```
>>>>line=f.readline() #read line by line from the file
```

```
>>>>while line: # till eof
```

```
>>>>print line #print the line
```

```
>>>> line=f.readline() #read line by line from the file
```

```
>>>>f.close() #close the file object
```

The while loop can be replaced using a for loop and the same result can be achieved.

The open() API can take two parameters, the first being the file name and the second the parameter to indicate the permission mode in which the file is opened—to read, write and execute.

For example, to write to a file, it needs to be opened with write permission as follows:

Sample Code

```
>>>>f.open("file1.txt",w)
```

```
>>>>f.write("hello!") #this writes the word "hello" to the file by name file1.txt.
```

```
>>>>f.write("Python    is    a    fantastic    language    to use.\ extremely easy for beginners to learn.\n")
```

```
>>>>f.close()
```

Now, if the file is opened, it will look like below.

hello! Python is a fantastic language to use.

Extremely easy for beginners to learn.

Note that the line starting with "extremely.." is printed in the second line—this is due to the newline format "escape sequence" used while writing to the file – '\n'. Several such escape sequences (a character preceded by \) defined in the language can be used to format how the output appears in a file or any other standard output.

Other common operations that can be performed on the file object are the following:

Operation	Description
f.closed()	Returns a Boolean: true if the file is closed, or false if it isn't.
f.mode()	Returns the access mode with which the file has been opened—it will either say read or write, etc.
f.name()	This method returns the name of the file object.
f.tell()	Used to tell the current position of the pointer in the file.
f.seek(x,y)	Used to move the pointer to a required position defined by the x, y position.

In addition, predefined functions available in the "os" module, such as renaming and deleting files can be used on os objects. In addition, Python provides several API to achieve common file operations provided by Linux commands such as mkdir to create a new directory or chdir to change directory path, etc.

For example:

import os #imports the os module

os.getcwd(); # gives the current working directory

Knowing how to use efficient files helps in writing many Python scripts useful to any programmer every day.

Practice Exercise

For practice, you need to perform the following tasks:

- Create a new file named test.txt.

- Write the entire practice exercise instructions on the file.

- Close the file and reopen it.

- Read the file and set the cursor back to 0.

- Close the file and open it using append access mode.

- Add a rewritten version of these instructions at the end of the file.

- Create a new file and put similar content to it by copying the contents of the test.txt file.

Chapter 11:

Object-Oriented Programming

Background and Concepts

Your Python programs process data. They succeed if the data is structured. You reserve some memory storage space, give it a name and fill this space with the contents. Exactly this happens in your Python program when you define a variable and assign it a specific value.

Until now, the data type did not play such a large role. Thanks to Python's dynamic type assignment the Python Core Engine decided while interpreting your code that data type to use internally. Used are, for example, whole numbers (integers) or numbers with decimal places (float), but also strings and logical values (True or False).

Object orientation is the independent setting of an extended, more complex data type.

This is made up of a number of basic data type variables. The objective behind this is to be able to depict the frequently complex reality or environment more easily in the form of a data structure. This achieves an abstraction level that corresponds with the Human conceptual world. This is a methodology to express reality more comprehensible in bits and bytes.

Object-Oriented Programming with Python

As we now know, the Python language is object-oriented, with the programs structured into classes and objects, which are instances of classes that encapsulate data and methods that operate on these data.

A sample Python program using class and function can be defined using the following syntax:

import module

class MyClass:

#comments, variable declaration

def func1():

#function definition

def func2():

#function definition

The first statement is used to "import" modules/packages that contain predefined functions, which can be used in our program.

The keyword "class" is used to notify the interpreter that this is the beginning of the class definition. Each class will contain a variable declaration that can be accessed via the objects/methods of the class. The methods/functions that can operate on these class variables are defined using the keyword "def." A function is nothing but a block of organized code that performs a specific action, and this block can be reused several times.

A function can take arguments as inputs and the "return" statement is used to exit/return from the block. The scope of variables declared within the function is local to that specific function.

An object of a given class can be declared using the following syntax,

Obj1 = MyClass(args)

Args are the arguments that can be passed to the constructor of the class, and by default, all classes by default have a constructor with the name __init__(self)

The obj1 can then be used to access the functions defined using the "." as follows:

Sample Code

Obj1.func1()

Sample Program:

```
class Employee:

#Variable Declaration

empNo = 0;

def __init__(self, fname, lname):

Employee.empNo += 1 #employee count

def dispName(self):

print self.fname+self.lname #concatenated first and last name
and prints that
```

emp1 = Employee("John ", "Bean") # creates an employee object

emp2 = Employee("Anne", "Hathway") #creates another employee object

emp1.dispName() #calls function using. operator to display name

emp2.dispName()

print "Total Count: %d" %Employee.empNo #prints count

Save the above code in a file, say sample1.py and executing the same will print the following output

>>>python sample1.py

John Bean

Anne Hathway

2

The above is a very simple example of writing a Python program using classes—basically, we concatenated the first and last name of the employees and printed the output to the console.

The first function defined in the class __init__() is called a constructor, and it is used to initialize objects. The statements:

emp1 = Employee("","")

Create an object with the respective values. In the above, note that a keyword "self" is passed as an argument to the functions. This is just a python convention; whether one uses this or not, this will not change the functioning of a given program, as it is used for the readability of the code.

The functions of a class can be accessed either by using the "." operator or simply using the parentheses.

Basic Knowledge about Classes

General Information

The object-oriented programming is a class of the highest level of abstraction and is, therefore, a category of objects. The name of a class denotes the complex data structure and thus the definition of your own data type. It contains variables—here called attributes—and functions—here called methods.

A new class can be determined via the keyword class, followed by an identifier that uniquely identifies the class. To derive the class from another already existing class, you additionally need the identifier of the base class in round parentheses.

Below you will see the creation of two classes—Room and Hotel. While the classroom is independent, the class Hotel is dependent on the already existing class Building.

class Room:

the following definitions belong to class Room

pass

class Hotel (Building):

the following definitions belong to class Hotel

pass

The spelling of a class name (identifier) follows certain rules. The class name always starts with an initial capital letter and has no underlines. A mixed use of upper—and lower—case letters is permitted (see [PEP8] and [HitchhikerStyle]).

Public and Private Attributes

A class can have class-specific variables. These variables are called attributes. Python does not distinguish between public and private attributes—C++ and Java do. Therefore, all defined attributes of a class in Python are publicly visible.

There is, however, an implicit distinction by a special identifier syntax. The identifier of a private attribute starts with an underline, such as _name.

class Room:

number = 0 # public attribute

_size = 42 # Attribute with a private identifier

Methods

The functions of a class are called methods. The definition of a method takes place analogous to the spelling of a Python function. After the keyword def, follows the identifier of the method, the reference to its own class (self), as well as the transferred parameters.

class Hotel:

rooms = 42 # preset that the hotel has 42 rooms

def countRooms (self):

"return the number of rooms that exist"

```
return self.rooms

def setRooms (self, numberOfRooms):

"set the number of rooms"

self.rooms = numberOfRooms

return

# define a new instance of the Hotel class

newHotel = Hotel

# output the number of rooms

print(newHotel.countRooms())

# set the number of rooms to 30

newHotel.setRooms(30)
```

The previous example defines a class named Hotel, which possesses an attribute rooms. From there follow the two methods countRooms and setRooms.

The countRooms method returns only the value of the room attribute to the caller. To do this, it uses the reference pointer self to access the attribute and returns its current value as the return value of the method. With the help of the setRooms() method, you set the value of the rooms attribute to the value given to the method setRooms() as a parameter.

After those two methods, an object called newHotel of type Hotel is defined. Thereafter call the previously defined methods countRooms() and setRooms(). Between the name of the object and the called method you need to write a dot . as a separator.

Initialize a Class

If you create a variable from the data type of a class, it occurs an instantiation of the object—it is newly created internally by Python.

To ensure that all the attributes of the new object possess the required values, Python runs when creating the object, a so-called constructor method. This only happens if this method in this class has been defined by you. This constructor method always takes the reserved name __init__. __init__() has at least one parameter named self. Use additional parameters to initialize object-related attributes properly.

The following is the procedure for the class Hotel. Originally, the attribute hotelName contains an empty string. With the definition of the variable newHotel it initiates the instantiation of the class. The method __init__() is executed here and the hotel name will be set to the new value *Grand Hotel*.

class Hotel:

hotelName = ""

def __init__(self, name):

"initialize the Hotel class object"

self.hotelName = name

return

newHotel = Hotel ("Grand Hotel")

The opposite of the constructor of a class is the destructor. The destructor holds the reserved identifier __del__. You use it to remove an object from memory and to clean up explicitly.

def __del__(self):

"remove the Hotel class object"

return

Python uses this method as its own keyword. Therefore, the call of the destructor is somewhat different from usual—del followed by the name of the object being removed.

del newHotel

Like the method __init__() introduced earlier, this method is not mandatory for their class. If it is not in their class, the Garbage Collector of the Python Core Engine will clean these objects up finally at the end of the program. However, if the classes you use are big or if you use many objects, it would be better to clean up regularly. This relieves the Garbage Collector on one side and creates storage space on the other.

Detailed Example

The following example shows a complete application using the example of a Hotel class. Three classes are used — Building, Hotel and Room. Building forms, the basic class on which the class Hotel is composed on. This building contains all the basic features of a building, where only the address is designed as an attribute.

class Building:

address = ""

```
def __init__(self, address):

"initialize the Building class object"

self.address = address

return
```

The Hotel class is a special building variant and possesses both attributes hotelName and hotelRooms as well as various methods. This makes it possible to add rooms and determine the number of rooms that are still available for rent.

```
class Hotel (Building):

hotelName = ""

hotelRooms = []

def __init__(self, address, name):

"initialize the Hotel class object"

self.address = address

self.hotelName = name

return

def __del__(self):

"remove the Hotel class object"

Return

def getName (self):

"return the hotel name"

return self.hotelName
```

```python
def getAddress (self):
"return the hotel address"
return self.address
def countHotelRooms (self):
"return the number of hotel rooms"
return len(self.hotelRooms)
def addHotelRoom (self, roomData):
"extend the room list by a room"
self.hotelRooms.append(roomData)
def countHotelRoomsAvailable (self):
"count the number of rooms that are available"
number = 0
for room in self.hotelRooms:
if room.isAvailable():
number += 1
return number
def isSingleRoomAvailable (self):
"""check if a one-bed room is available
return the room number, otherwise 0"""
for room in self.hotelRooms:
if room.isAvailable():
```

```
if room.hasBeds() == 1:

return room.getRoomNumber()

return 0
```

The Room class is again separate and represents all characteristics of a room. As attributes are the room number, the availability of a room—free or occupied—as well as the number of beds that are placed in the room. At the same time, methods were implemented that determine, for example, whether a room is available and that room number it has. Using the methods book() and release(), a room is occupied or space is released again.

```
class Room:

number = 0

availability = True

beds = 1

def __init__(self, number, availability, beds):

"initialize the room information"

self.number = number

self.availability = availability

self.beds = beds

return

def isAvailable (self):

"check if a room is available"

return self.availability
```

```python
def getRoomNumber (self):

"return the room number"

return self.number

def book (self):

"book the room"

self.availability = False

return

def release (self):

"release the room"

self.availability = True

return

def hasBeds (self):

"return the number of beds in the room"

return self.beds
```

Now the application of the previously defined classes is still missing.

This is what happens now.

Step 1 is the definition of the hotel with its address and name. In step 2, three rooms are defined, which are added to the room list of the hotel. In step 3, you determine the number of rooms as well as the number of free rooms. In Step 4 it clarifies the question, whether a single room is available at the moment or not.

- **Define hotel data.**

newHotel = Hotel ("2 Old Harbour Road, Bornemouth", "Grand Hotel")

print (newHotel.getName())

print (newHotel.getAddress())

- **Define a two-bed room.**

room1 = Room (1, True, 2)

newHotel.addHotelRoom (room1)

- **Define a four-bed room, occupied.**

room2 = Room (2, False, 4)

newHotel.addHotelRoom (room2)

- **Define a single-bed room.**

room3 = Room (3, True, 1)

newHotel.addHotelRoom (room3)

- **Count the number of rooms.**

print ("total rooms: %i" % newHotel.countHotelRooms())

- **How many rooms are available, currently?**

print ("available rooms: %i" % newHotel.countHotelRoomsAvailable())

- **Is a single room available?**

print ("single room available (room number):" , newHotel.isSingleRoomAvailable())

Save the above source code as a Python program called hotel.py. Then run it and you will get the following output:
$ python3 hotel.py

- **Grand Hotel**

2 Old Harbor Road, Bornemouth

total rooms: 3

available rooms: 2

single room available (room number): 3

$

1.3. Building Classes for Advanced Users

Deriving Classes

Create a class based on a class that already exists. The technical term for this is the derivation of a class. To do this, type in the class definition extended by the name of the existing class (called the *basic class* or *upper class*).

class Building:

pass

class Hotel (Building):

pass

class Busstop (Building):

pass

In this step, the derived class inherits everything from the base class, all methods and attributes. The following example demonstrates this more precisely. The class Busstop only gets a single new attribute called buslines — everything else remains the same for now.

```
class Building:

address = ""

def __init __ (self, address):

"initialize the building class"

self.address = address

return

def getAddress (self):

"return the address of the building"

return self.address

def __str__ (self):

"output the data of the building object"

outputString = "Building at% s"% self.getAddress ()

return outputString

class Busstop (Building):

buslines = []
```

Now we test the objects of those two classes. Therefore, we create an object of the class Building and an object of the class Busstop as follows: building = Building ("2 Albert Road")

```
print (building)
```

```
busstop = Busstop ("15 Lower Main Road")
```

```
print (busstop)
```

Save the above program in the file busstop.py. Afterwards run it and you will get the following output:

```
$ python3 busstop.py
```

building at 2 Albert Road

building at 15 Lower Main Road

```
$
```

It shows that in both cases the method ___str ___() is derived from the class Building. In each case the corresponding address is displayed which is stored in the object.

Overloading methods

In the example in the previous section, the output was for both objects almost identical. To change this, overwrite the already existing method. This process is also called method "overloading." To do this, you define a method in the derived class with the same name.

```
def ___str___ (self):
```

"output the data of the busstop object"

```
position = "busstop at %s"% self.getAddress ()
```

return position

The instantiation of the objects and the call up of the methods remains identical to before. The results after the execution of the modified program with the adapted class Busstop looks as follows: $ python3 busstop.py

building at 2 Albert Road

busstop at 15 Lower Main Road

$

Chapter 12:

Dictionaries

Dictionaries are data types in the Python programming language that is much similar to a list of certain objects contained in a particular collection. Let us venture into some of the similar characteristics and differences that lists, and dictionaries share, so as to get the basic idea of what dictionaries are all about. Similar characteristics of these two data types include: They are both mutable, hence due to any shifting at any particular moment of time, they are dynamic. They are able to change in a way that they are to grow and shrink during any episodes and a dictionary is capable of containing another dictionary in it, and a list is too able to contain another list in it hence concluding that these data types can be nested. The only difference between these two data types comes from how the data values are accessed. Lists are normally accessed by various indexing operations whereas dictionaries are basically accessed by the use of various kinds of keys.

Dictionaries basically consist of some key-value pairs that normally are the key to a specified associated value. We define a dictionary in Python by first enclosing the entire list using curly brackets, placing a full colon that separates the key pairs to the associated value placed, and lastly by using a comma mark in separating the various kinds of key pairs that are available in the dictionary. Another way in which dictionaries can be constructed in the Python world is through the use of dict() function in the program. This one works in a way that the value of the argument in the dict() function consists of the keys and the respective values that have been paired along with it. Kindly remember that square brackets are normally used to contain the key-value pairs in the program in question. Once dictionaries have been defined, it is possible to display its contents where they get displayed just the same way they were defined in a structural manner.

Dictionaries are accessed by specifying its relevant key inside square brackets symbol, and in a case where a certain key does not exist in a particular dictionary, an exception is raised right away as an error made. It is then possible to add a certain entry in a particular dictionary where a new key with its value is assigned in the program. In updating a particular entry, a new value is just assigned to an existing key. During the delete of an entry operation, a del statement is normally used specifying the actual key to delete.

Lastly, methods and various operations are normally implemented in dictionaries so various tasks can be achieved. For example, if a developer has the intention of copying a particular dictionary, he or she is obligated to use the copy() method of the Python programming language.

Some of the other methods include:

Clear method

this method clears all the kinds of elements that are present in the dictionary.

Get method

this one gives the value of the key that has been specified in the dictionary.

From keys

this kind of method gives out a particular amount of keys and values from the dictionary.

Keys

outputs a list that entails the keys in the dictionary.

Pop

this method removes the elements with the specified keys.

Value method

this method gives out a collection of all the values that are present in a certain dictionary.

A dictionary object represents a hash table as a collection of key-value pairs. The dictionary is also a builtin data type, with the difference between a list and dictionary being that the former is an organized array while the latter is an unorganized collection, which means the values are not accessed using indices but by using the 'key' value. However, like lists, dictionaries are dynamic and can be of variable length.

Declaration:

dict1 = {key1:value1, key2:value2, key3:value3.... }

The dictionary elements are enclosed with flower brackets, with each key-value pair separated by a colon and with the pairs separated by commas.

Just like lists, tuples can be concatenated, repeated, sliced, indexed, iterated and length found, but operations like insert/delete are not possible as tuples are immutable.

However, it is possible to concatenate two tuples and save it in a third tuple, like the following

>>> tup2 = ("Hello","World", 2000, 1990)

>>> tup1 = (1,2,3,4,5)

>>> tup3 = tup1 + tup2

>>> print tup3

(1, 2, 3, 4, 5, 'Hello', 'World', 2000, 1990)

Some builtin functions, which can be used on tuples, include comparing two tuples and finding the min, max in elements of the tuple:

>>> print tup1

(1, 2, 3, 4, 5)

>>> max(tup1)

5

>>> min(tup1)

1

The compare method returns the value 0 if the tuples match and -1 if they do not:

>>> print tup1

(1, 2, 3, 4, 5)

>>> print tup4

(1, 2, 3, 4, 5)

>>> cmp(tup1,tup4)

0

>>> print tup2

('Hello', 'World', 2000, 1990)

>>> cmp(tup1,tup2)

-1

You can also convert a list to a tuple using the following function

>>> print a

[1, 2, 3, 4, 5]

>>> tuple(a)

(1, 2, 3, 4, 5)

Conclusion

Thank you for reading this book. I hope this book was able to help you to understand what Python computer programming language is and how it works. Once you get to know it, Python is very easy to learn and is one of the most satisfying languages in terms of writing programs.

Every measure was taken into consideration to ensure that all the chapters give you detailed and easy to understand information. I intentionally used simple language throughout the book to make sure that you are empowered after reading. The book has deliberately avoided sophisticated theories and stuck to simple explanations that you can use at your convenience when studying.

There are a lot of other coding languages out there that you are able to work with, but Python is one of the best that works for most beginner programmers, providing the power and the ease of use that you are looking for when you first get started in this kind of coding language. This guidebook took the time to explore how Python works and some of the different types of coding that you can do with it.

In addition to seeing a lot of examples of how you can code in Python and how you can create some of your programs in this language, we also spent some time looking at how to work with Python when it comes to the world of machine learning, artificial intelligence, and data analysis. These are topics and parts of technology that are taking off and many programmers are trying to learn more about it, and with the help of this guidebook, you will be able to handle all of these, even as a beginner in Python.

Programming is one of the most liberating tasks known to man because it's the ultimate art form. It's the most interactive art form too. When you program, what you're doing is literally talking to the computer, thereby making the computer talk to the user. Every single program you make is an extension of the effort you put into it and the time and code you've dedicated to it.

Remember going forward that without a doubt, it will not always be easy. It won't be even remotely easy. Programming is made difficult by its very nature. Humans, we just don't think like computers.

The next step is to stop reading and start applying the lessons you have learned in real life. Do whatever you have identified as necessary to improve applications of programming in real life. You will realize that the majority of those who seem to have it all together lack the basic Python programming skills. Try to engage them and teach them a thing or two you have learned herein. You may even recommend or gift this book to them.

You can take your learning further. There are plenty of tutorials on the Internet and lots of courses that you can sign up for. There are also a lot of forums where a friendly and helpful community is ready to help you solve any problems you may have and help you to get ahead in programming. The most important thing is to practice; things are changing all the time in Python and, if you don't keep up with it, you will find you have to start over again.

Thank you and good luck!

www.ingramcontent.com/pod-product-compliance
Lightning Source LLC
La Vergne TN
LVHW051242050326
832903LV00028B/2529